ESSENTIAL ELEMENTS®
FOR BAND
COMPREHENSIVE BAND METHOD

TIM LAUTZENHEISER
PAUL LAVENDER

JOHN HIGGINS
TOM C. RHODES

CHARLES MENGHINI
DON BIERSCHENK

These piano accompaniments can provide helpful guidance for teaching beginning instrumentalists. The format includes a cue line to provide the director or pianist with a visual guide of the student melody part.

The harmony and style of each piano example are fully compatible with the online audio accompaniment tracks included with each student book.

Each example also includes chord symbols for the director or pianist to adapt the written part as needed for specific teaching situations.

ISBN 978-0-634-00329-5

HAL•LEONARD®

Visit Hal Leonard Online at
www.halleonard.com

Contact us:
Hal Leonard
7777 West Bluemound Road
Milwaukee, WI 53213
Email: info@halleonard.com

In Europe, contact:
Hal Leonard Europe Limited
42 Wigmore Street
Marylebone, London, W1U 2RN
Email: info@halleonardeurope.com

In Australia, contact:
Hal Leonard Australia Pty. Ltd.
4 Lentara Court
Cheltenham, Victoria, 3192 Australia
Email: info@halleonard.com.au

1. THE FIRST NOTE

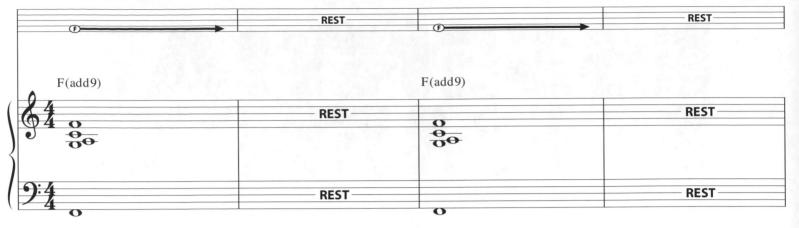

2. COUNT AND PLAY

3. A NEW NOTE

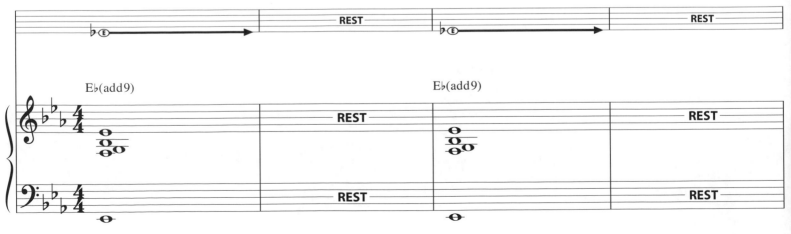

4. TWO'S A TEAM

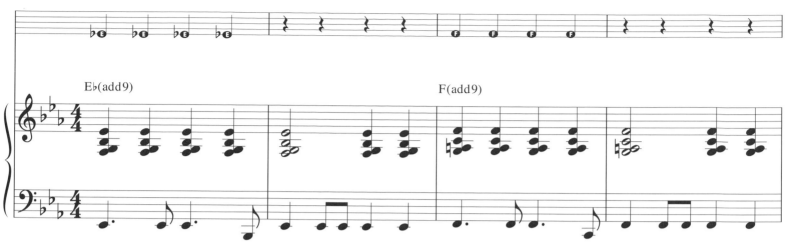

5. HEADING DOWN

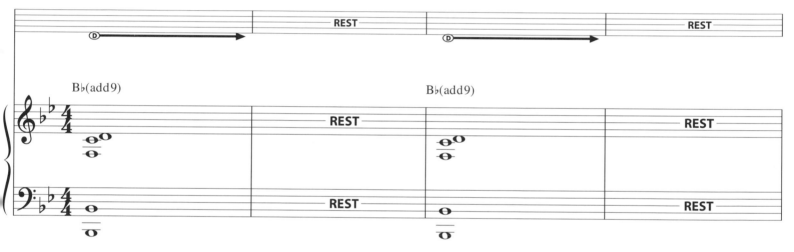

6. MOVING ON UP

7. THE LONG HAUL

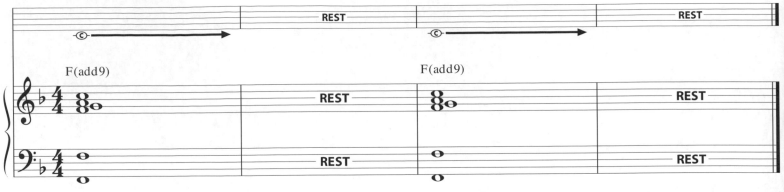

8. FOUR BY FOUR

Student books have repeats,
not 1st and 2nd endings (until ex. 76).

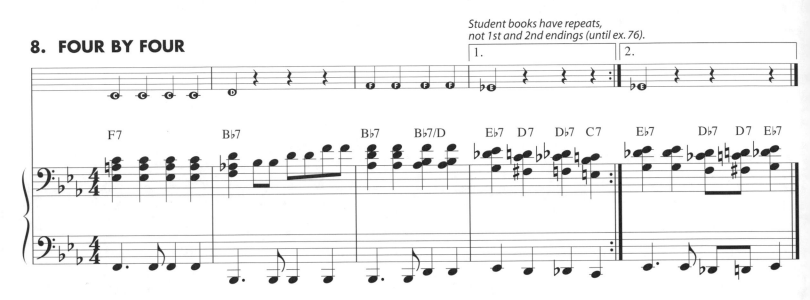

9. TOUCHDOWN

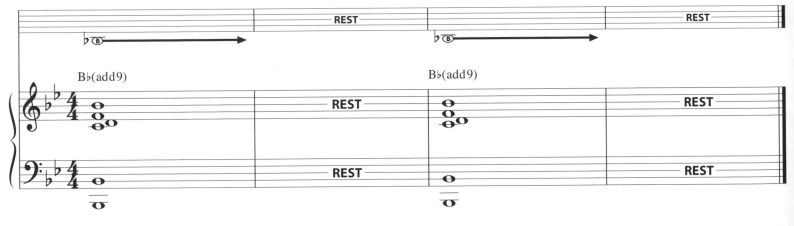

10. THE FAB FIVE

11. READING THE NOTES

12. FIRST FLIGHT

13. ESSENTIAL ELEMENTS QUIZ

14. ROLLING ALONG

15. RHYTHM RAP

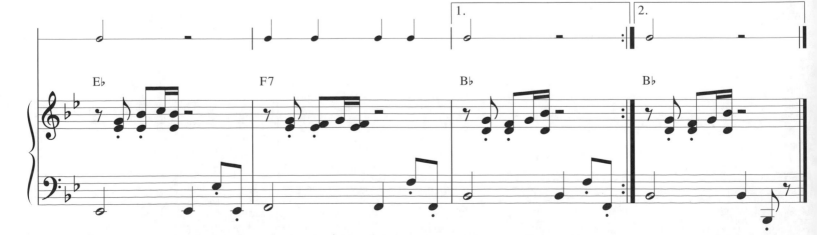

16. THE HALF COUNTS

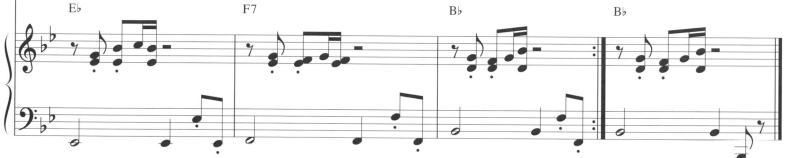

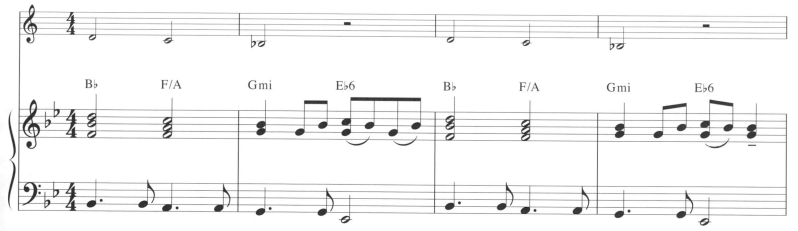

17. HOT CROSS BUNS

18. GO TELL AUNT RHODIE

American Folk Song

19. ESSENTIAL ELEMENTS QUIZ

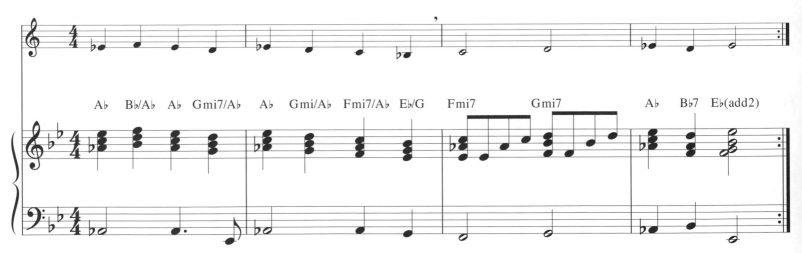

20. RHYTHM RAP

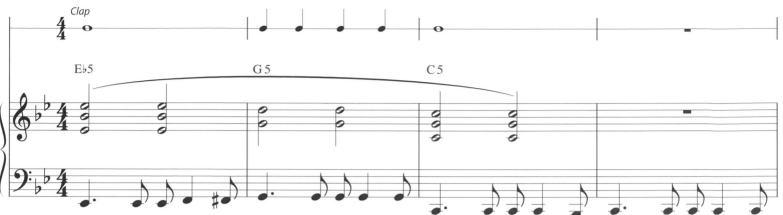

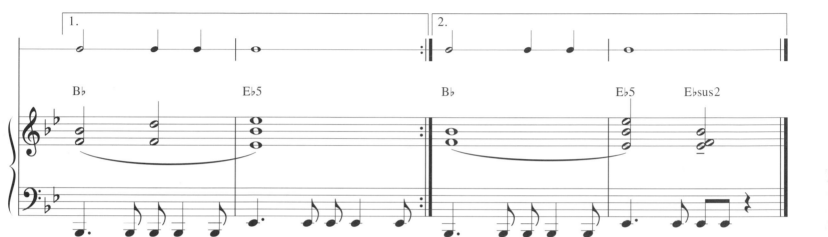

21. THE WHOLE THING

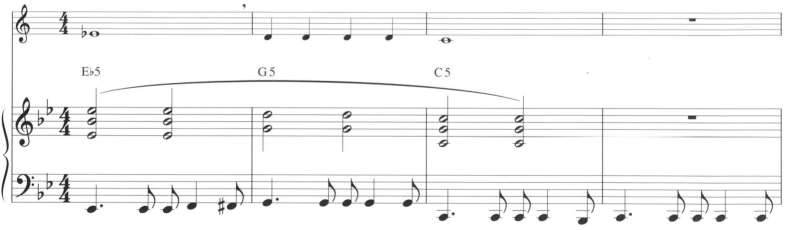

22. SPLIT DECISION – Duet

23. MARCH STEPS

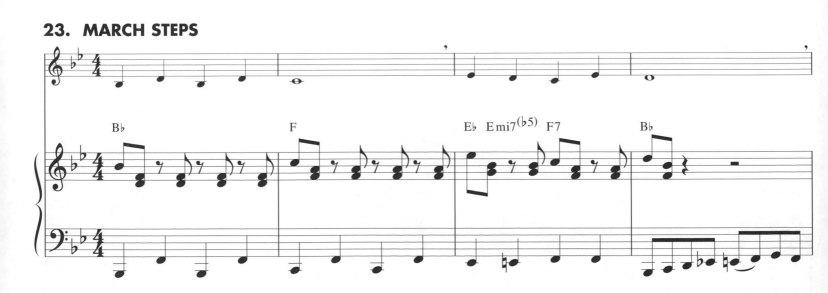

24. LISTEN TO OUR SECTIONS

25. LIGHTLY ROW

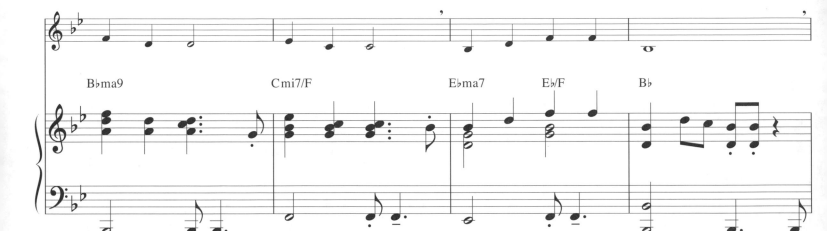

26. ESSENTIAL ELEMENTS QUIZ

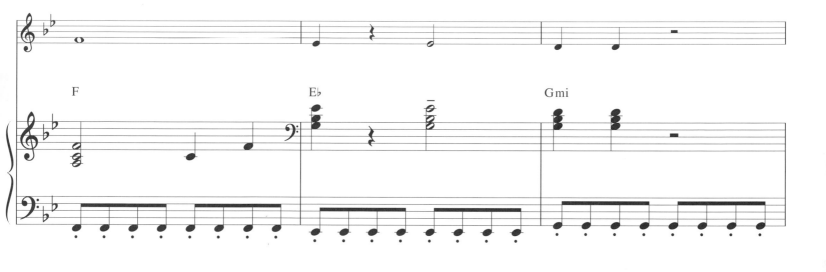

27. REACHING HIGHER

28. AU CLAIRE DE LA LUNE

French Folk Song

29. REMIX

30. LONDON BRIDGE – Duet

English Folk Song

31. A MOZART MELODY

Adaptation

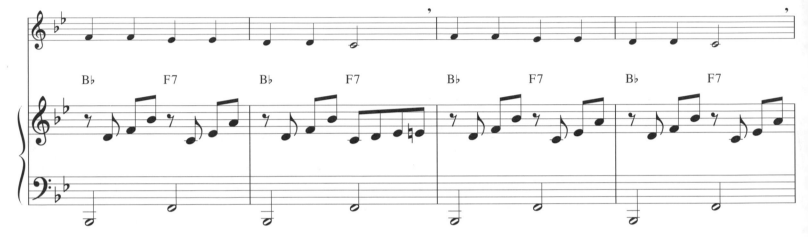

32. ESSENTIAL ELEMENTS QUIZ

33. DEEP POCKETS

34. DOODLE ALL DAY

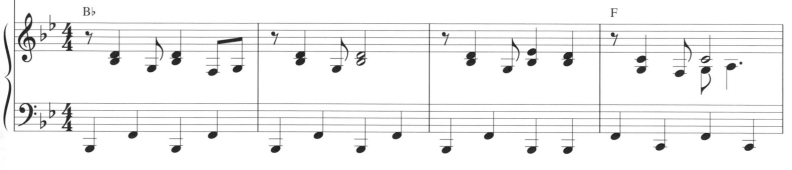

35. JUMP ROPE

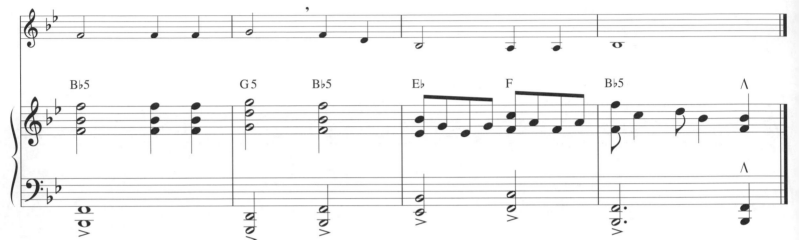

36. A-TISKET, A-TASKET

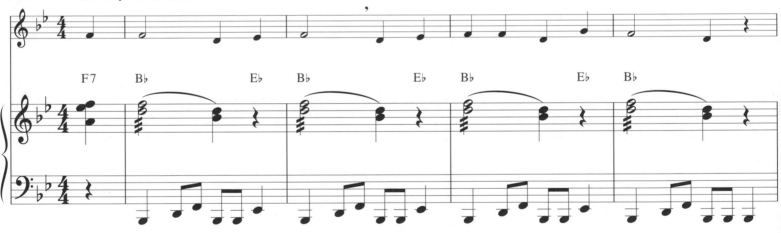

37. LOUD AND SOFT

38. JINGLE BELLS

J. S. Pierpont

39. MY DREYDL

Traditional Hanukkah Song

22

40. RHYTHM RAP

41. EIGHTH NOTE JAM

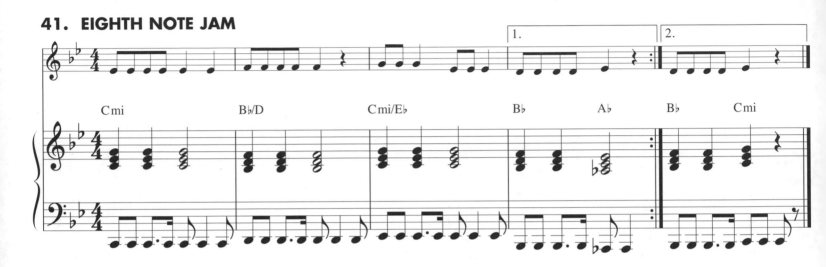

42. SKIP TO MY LOU

American Folk Song

43. LONG, LONG AGO

44. OH, SUSANNA

Stephen Collins Foster

45. ESSENTIAL ELEMENTS QUIZ – WILLIAM TELL

Gioacchino Rossini

46. RHYTHM RAP

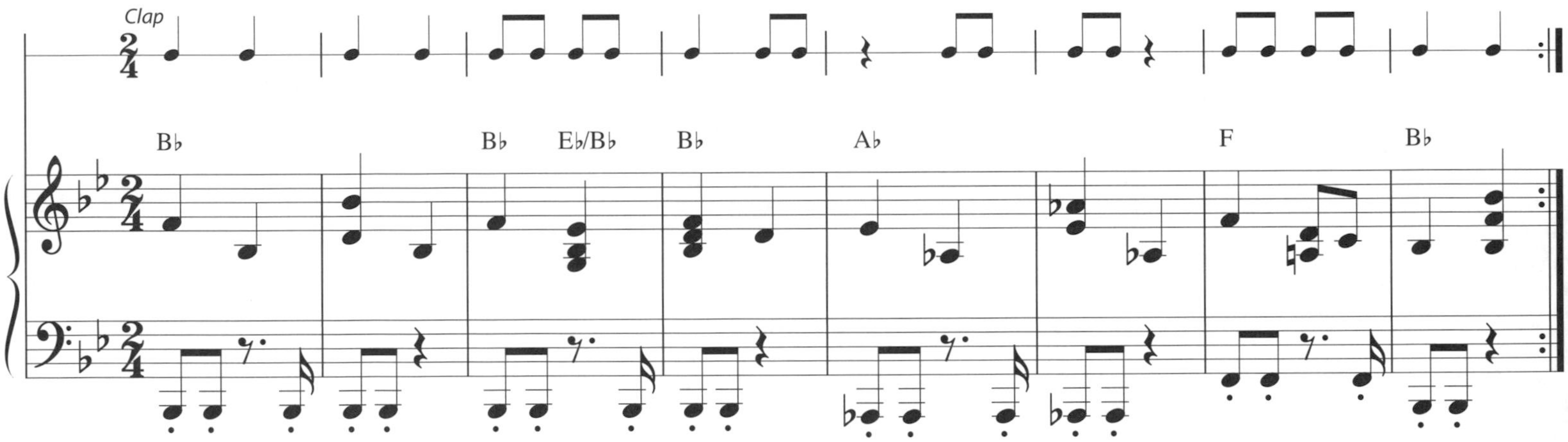

47. TWO BY TWO

48. HIGH SCHOOL CADETS – March

John Philip Sousa

49. HEY, HO! NOBODY'S HOME

50. CLAP THE DYNAMICS

51. PLAY THE DYNAMICS

52. PERFORMANCE WARM-UPS

TONE BUILDER

RHYTHM ETUDE

RHYTHM RAP

CHORALE

53. AURA LEE – Duet or Band Arrangement

George R. Poulton

54. FRÈRE JACQUES – Round   *(When group A reaches ② group B begins at ①)*

French Folk Song

55. WHEN THE SAINTS GO MARCHING IN – Band Arrangement

Arr. by John Higgins

56. OLD MACDONALD HAD A BAND – Section Feature

57. ODE TO JOY (from Symphony No. 9)

Ludwig van Beethoven
Arr. by John Higgins

58. HARD ROCK BLUES – Encore

John Higgins

59. FIT TO BE TIED

60. ALOUETTE

French-Canadian Folk Song

61. ALOUETTE – THE SEQUEL   French-Canadian Folk Song

62. CAMPTOWN RACES

Stephen Collins Foster

63. NEW DIRECTIONS

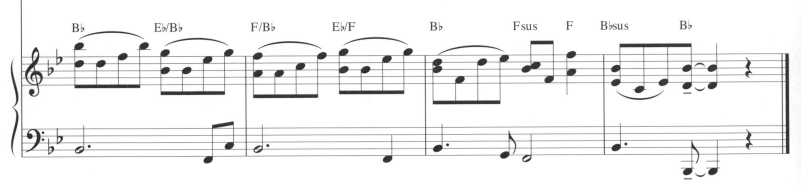

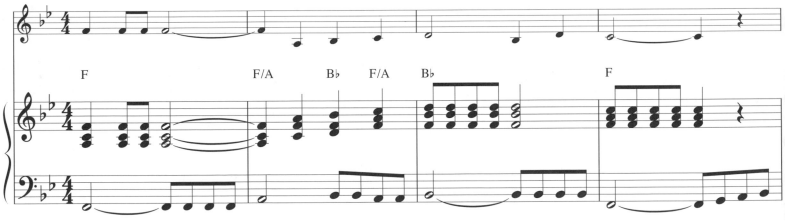

64. THE NOBLES

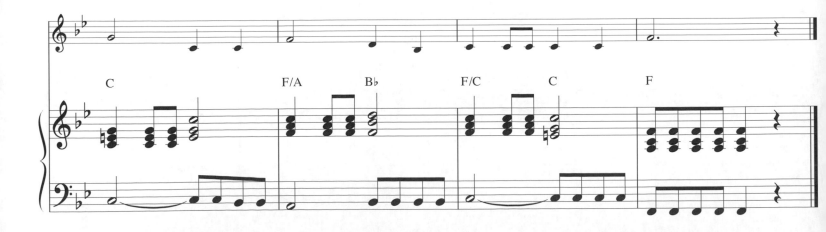

65. ESSENTIAL ELEMENTS QUIZ

66. RHYTHM RAP

67. THREE BEAT JAM

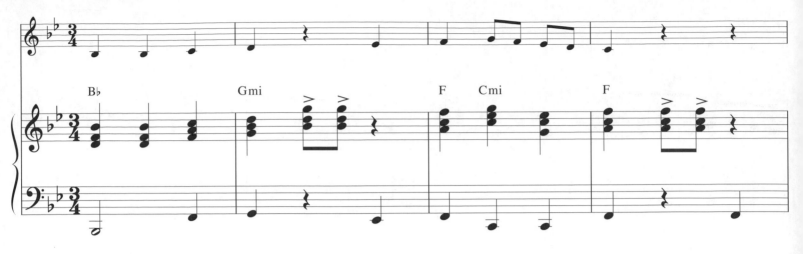

68. BARCAROLLE

Jacques Offenbach

69. MORNING (from Peer Gynt)

Edvard Grieg

70. ACCENT YOUR TALENT

71. MEXICAN CLAPPING SONG ("Chiapanecas")

Latin American Folk Song

72. ESSENTIAL CREATIVITY – *Writing assignment in student books.*

73. HOT MUFFINS

74. COSSACK DANCE

Allegro

75. BASIC BLUES

76. HIGH FLYING

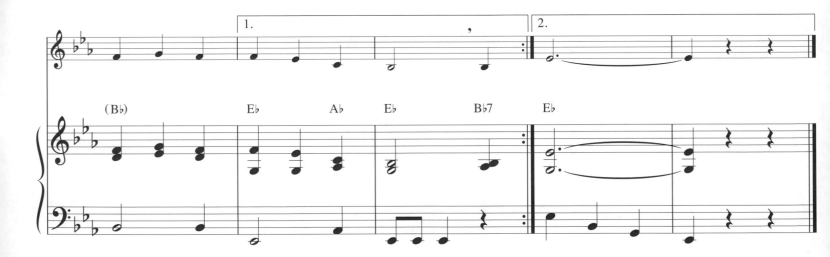

77. SAKURA, SAKURA – Band Arrangement

Japanese Folk Song
Arr. by John Higgins

44

78. UP ON A HOUSETOP

79. JOLLY OLD ST. NICK – Duet

Moderato

80. THE BIG AIRSTREAM

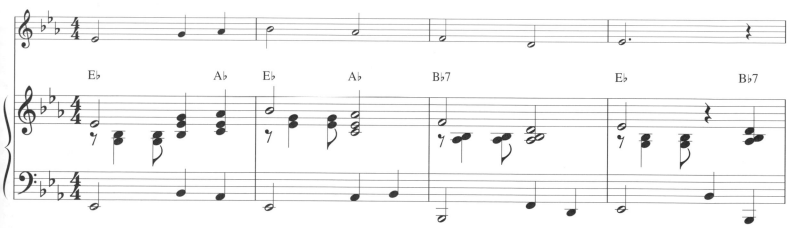

81. WALTZ THEME

Franz Lehar

82. AIR TIME

83. DOWN BY THE STATION

Student books have repeats, not 1st and 2nd endings.

84. ESSENTIAL ELEMENTS QUIZ

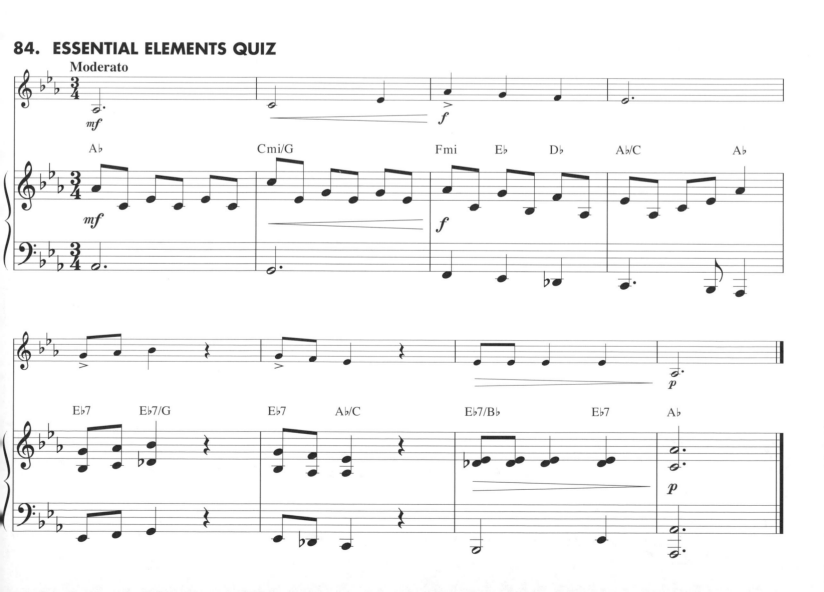

85. ESSENTIAL CREATIVITY   *Using these notes, improvise your own rhythms:*

86. TONE BUILDER

Student books have repeats, not 1st and 2nd endings.

87. RHYTHM BUILDER

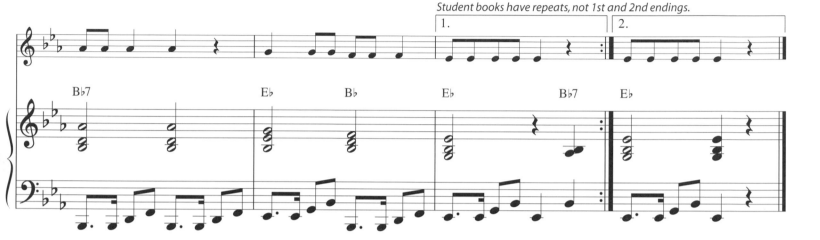

Student books have repeats, not 1st and 2nd endings.

1. 2.

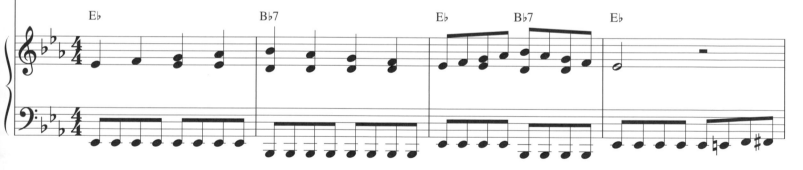

88. TECHNIQUE TRAX

Student books have repeats, not 1st and 2nd endings.

1. 2.

89. CHORALE *(Adapted from Cantata 147)*

Johann Sebastian Bach

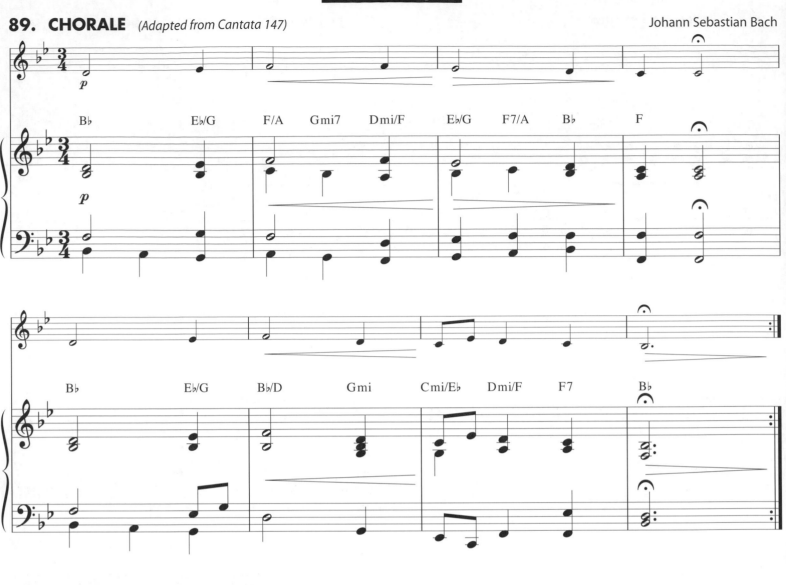

90. VARIATIONS ON A FAMILIAR THEME

91. BANANA BOAT SONG

Caribbean Folk Song

92. RAZOR'S EDGE

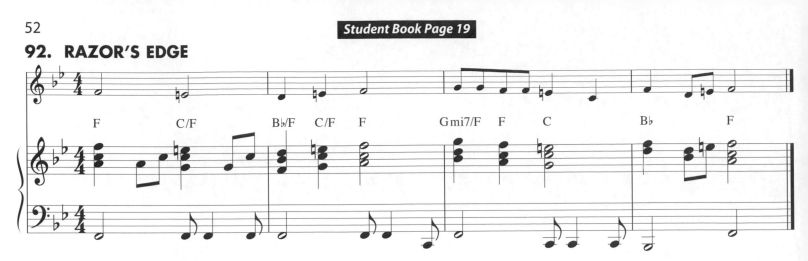

93. THE MUSIC BOX

94. EZEKIEL SAW THE WHEEL

African-American Spiritual

95. SMOOTH OPERATOR

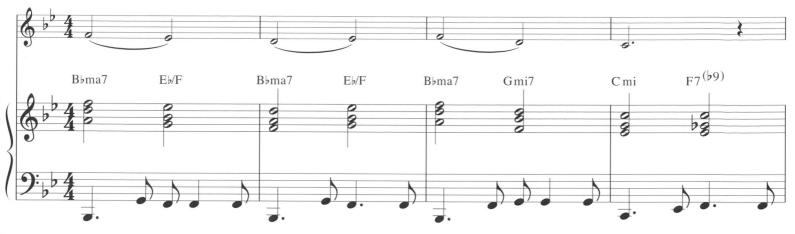

96. GLIDING ALONG

97. TROMBONE RAG

98. ESSENTIAL ELEMENTS QUIZ

Student books have a D.C. al Fine at measure 8 with the Fine at measure 4.

99. TAKE THE LEAD

100. THE COLD WIND

101. PHRASEOLOGY

102. SATIN LATIN

103. MINUET – Duet

Johann Sebastian Bach

104. ESSENTIAL CREATIVITY – *Writing assignment in student books.*

105. NATURALLY

106. MARCH MILITAIRE

Franz Schubert

107. THE FLAT ZONE

108. ON TOP OF OLD SMOKEY

American Folk Song

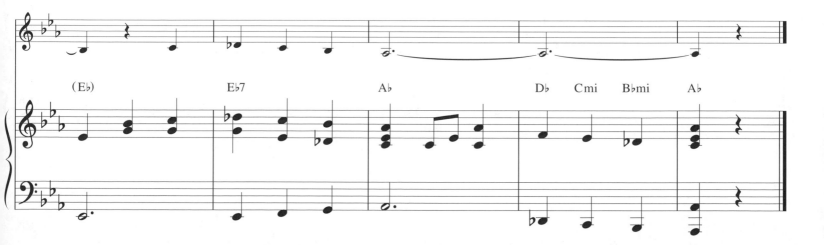

109. BOTTOM BASS BOOGIE – Duet

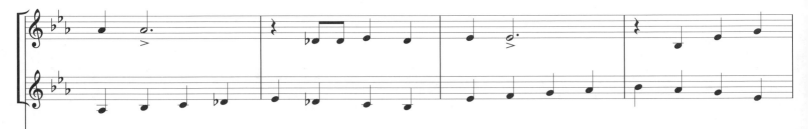

110. RHYTHM RAP

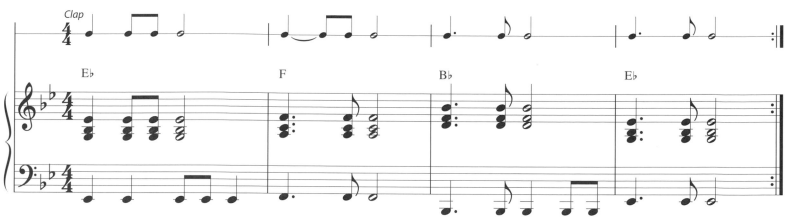

111. THE DOT ALWAYS COUNTS

112. ALL THROUGH THE NIGHT

113. SEA CHANTY

English Folk Song

114. SCARBOROUGH FAIR

English Folk Song

115. RHYTHM RAP

116. THE TURNAROUND

117. ESSENTIAL ELEMENTS QUIZ – AULD LANG SYNE

Scottish Folk Song

118. THEME FROM "NEW WORLD SYMPHONY"

Antonin Dvořák

119. GRENADILLA GORILLA JUMP No. 1

120. JUMPIN' UP AND DOWN

121. GRENADILLA GORILLA JUMP No. 2

122. JUMPIN' FOR JOY

68

123. GRENADILLA GORILLA JUMP No. 3

124. JUMPIN' JACKS

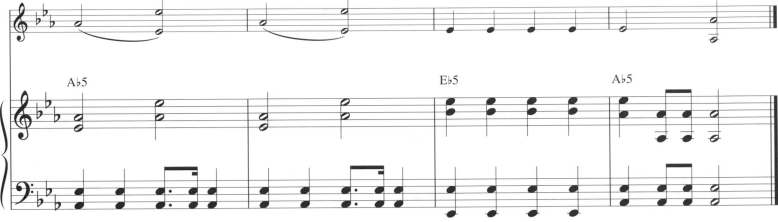

125. ESSENTIAL ELEMENTS QUIZ

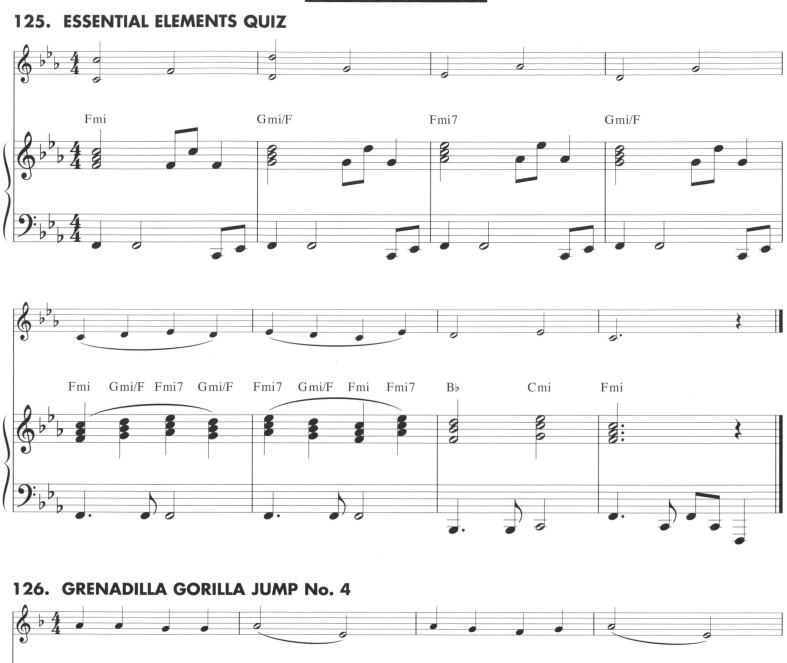

126. GRENADILLA GORILLA JUMP No. 4

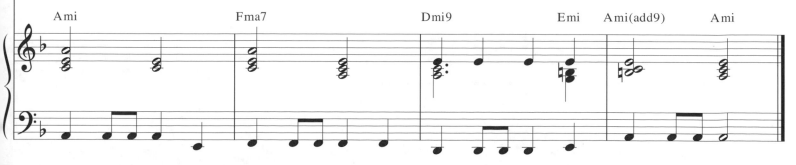

127. THREE IS THE COUNT

Student books have repeats, not 1st and 2nd endings.

128. GRENADILLA GORILLA JUMP No. 5

129. TECHNIQUE TRAX

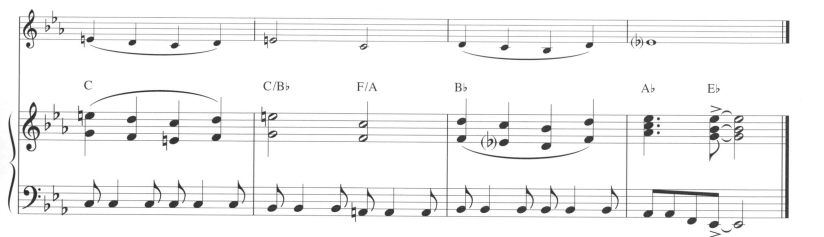

130. CROSSING OVER

131. KUM BAH YAH – Trio

African Folk Song

132. MICHAEL ROW THE BOAT ASHORE

African-American Spiritual

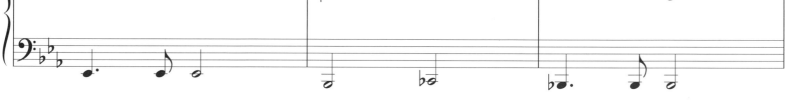

133. AUSTRIAN WALTZ

Austrian Folk Song

Student books have repeats, not 1st and 2nd endings.

134. BOTANY BAY

Australian Folk Song

135. TECHNIQUE TRAX

Student books have repeats, not 1st and 2nd endings.

136. FINLANDIA

Jean Sibelius

137. ESSENTIAL CREATIVITY

Create your own variations by penciling in a dot and a flag to change the rhythm of any measure from

138. EASY GORILLA JUMPS

139. TECHNIQUE TRAX

140. MORE TECHNIQUE TRAX

141. GERMAN FOLK SONG

142. THE SAINTS GO MARCHIN' AGAIN

James Black and Katherine Purvis

Allegro

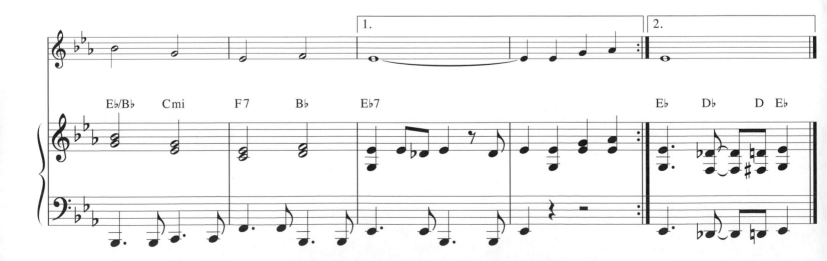

143. LOWLAND GORILLA WALK

144. SMOOTH SAILING

145. MORE GORILLA JUMPS

146. FULL COVERAGE

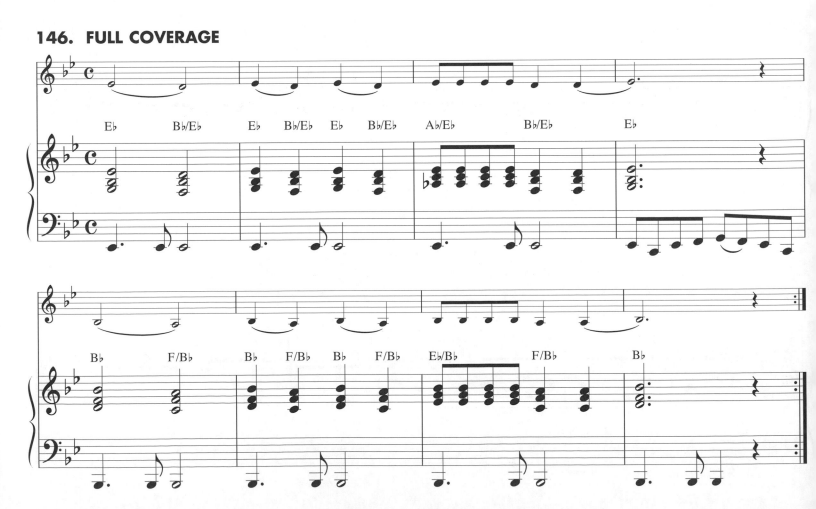

147. CONCERT B♭ SCALE

Student books have repeats, not 1st and 2nd endings.

148. IN HARMONY

Student books have repeats, not 1st and 2nd endings.

149. SCALE AND ARPEGGIO

Student books have repeats, not 1st and 2nd endings.

150. THEME FROM "SURPRISE SYMPHONY"

Franz Josef Haydn

151. ESSENTIAL ELEMENTS QUIZ – THE STREETS OF LAREDO

American Folk Song

152. SCHOOL SPIRIT – Band Arrangement

W.T. Purdy
Arr. by John Higgins

March Style

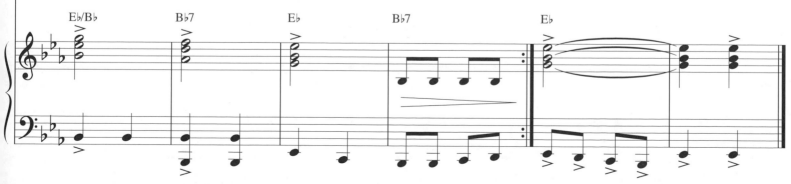

153. CARNIVAL OF VENICE – Band Arrangement

Julius Benedict
Arr. by John Higgins

154. RANGE AND FLEXIBILITY BUILDER

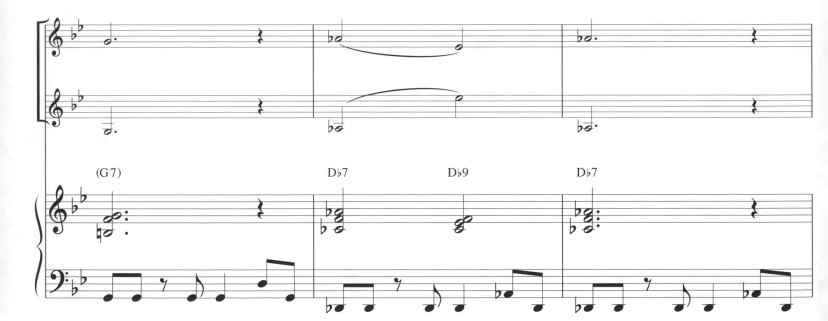

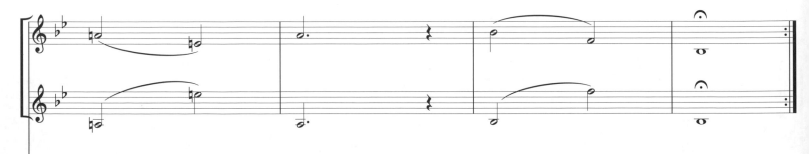

155. TECHNIQUE TRAX

156. CHORALE

Johann Sebastian Bach

157. HATIKVAH

Israeli National Anthem

158. RHYTHM RAP

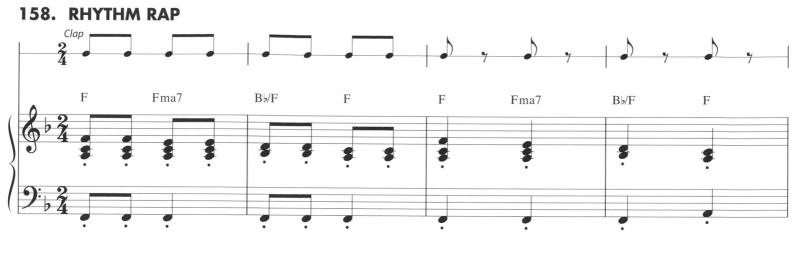

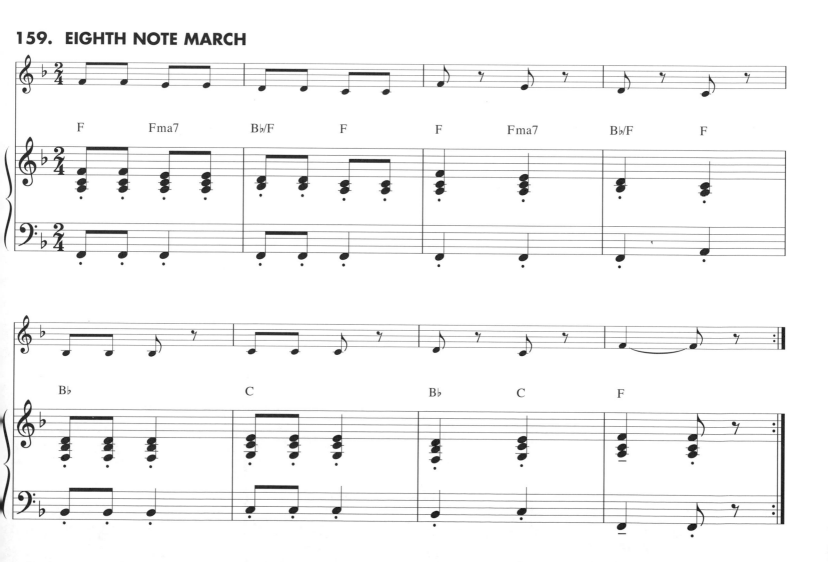

159. EIGHTH NOTE MARCH

160. MINUET

Johann Sebastian Bach

161. RHYTHM RAP

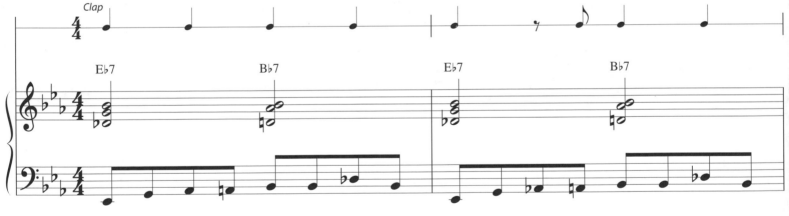

Student books have repeats, not 1st and 2nd endings.

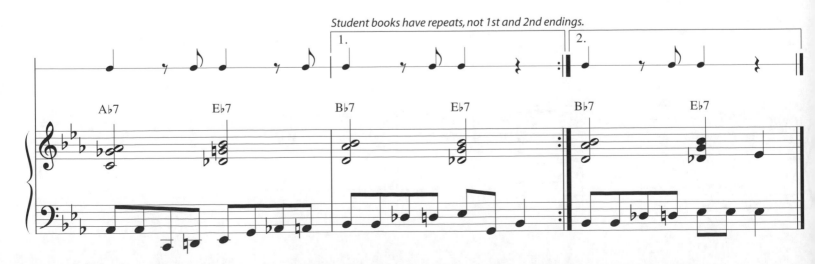

162. EIGHTH NOTES OFF THE BEAT

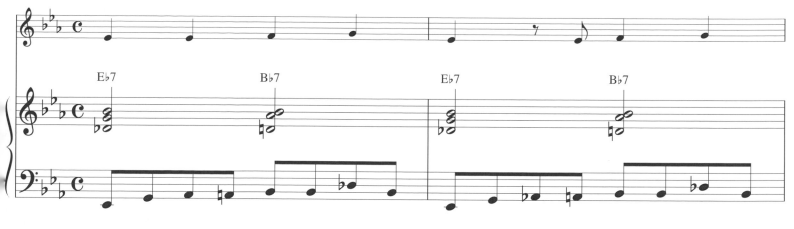

Student books have repeats, not 1st and 2nd endings.

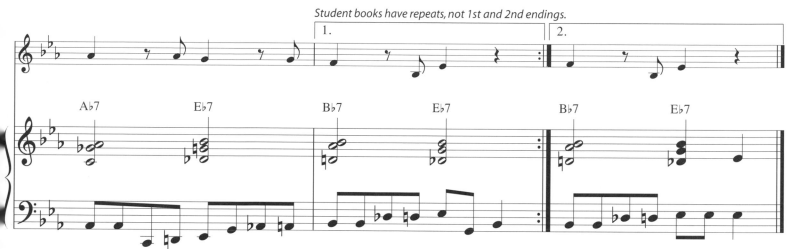

163. EIGHTH NOTE SCRAMBLE

164. ESSENTIAL ELEMENTS QUIZ

165. DANCING MELODY

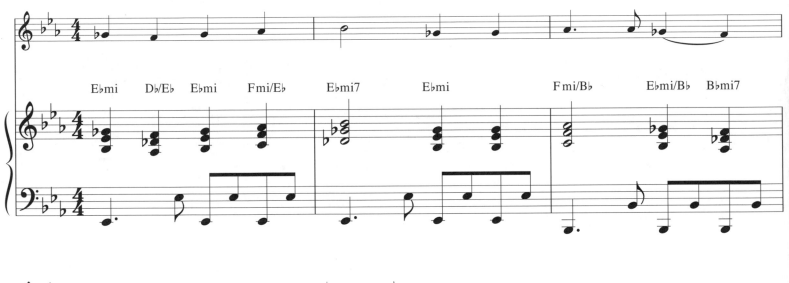

166. EL CAPITAN

John Philip Sousa

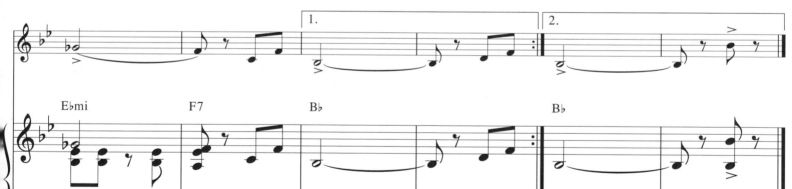

167. O CANADA

Calixa Lavallee,
l'Hon. Judge Routhier
and Justice R.S. Weir

Maestoso (Majestically)

168. ESSENTIAL ELEMENTS QUIZ – METER MANIA

169. SNAKE CHARMER

170. DARK SHADOWS

Student books have repeats, not 1st and 2nd endings.

171. CLOSE ENCOUNTERS

172. MARCH SLAV

Peter Illyich Tchaikovsky

173. NOTES IN DISGUISE

174. HALF-STEPPIN'

175. EGYPTIAN DANCE

Camille Saint-Saëns

176. SILVER MOON BOAT

Chinese Folk Song

177. THEME FROM SYMPHONY NO. 7 – Duet

Ludwig van Beethoven

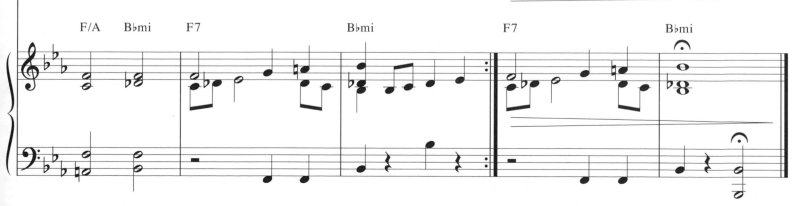

178. CAPRICCIO ITALIEN

Peter Illyich Tchaikovsky

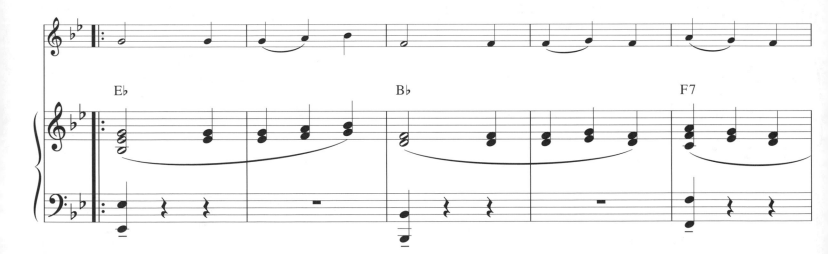

179. AMERICAN PATROL

F.W. Meacham

180. WAYFARING STRANGER

African-American Spiritual

181. ESSENTIAL ELEMENTS QUIZ – SCALE COUNTING CONQUEST

182. AMERICA THE BEAUTIFUL – Band Arrangement

Samuel A. Ward
Arr. by John Higgins

Fmi7   Bb7   Fmi7/C   Bb7/D   Bb7   Fmi/C   Bb7/D   Eb   Fmi7   Eb/G   Gb   Ab   Eb/G   Bb7/F   Eb   N.C.

Bb/D   Cmi   Cmi/Bb   Ab   Cmi7/G   Fmi7   Eb   Bb/D   Cmi7   Bb   N.C.

25 **Maestoso**

Bb   Eb

183. LA CUCARACHA – Band Arrangement

Latin Rock

Latin American Folk Song
Arr. by John Higgins

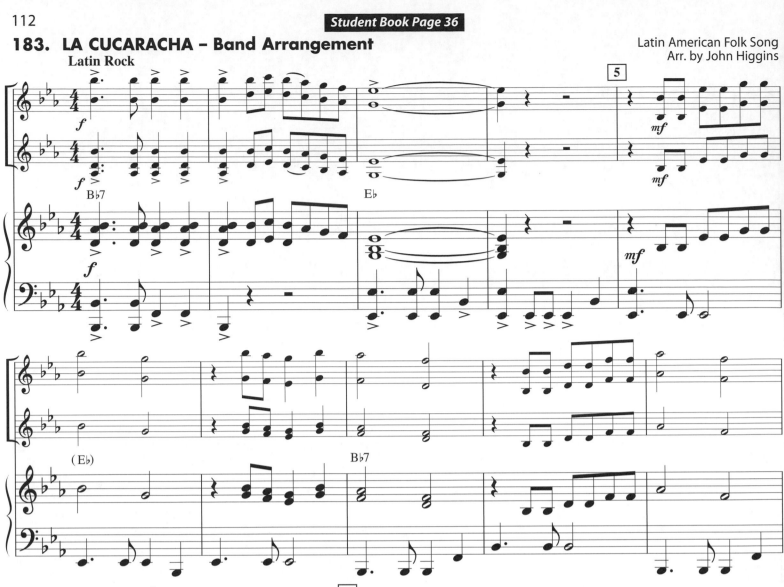

184. THEME FROM 1812 OVERTURE – Band Arrangement

Peter Illyich Tchaikovsky
Arr. by John Higgins

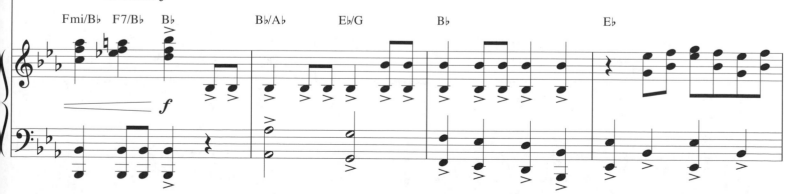

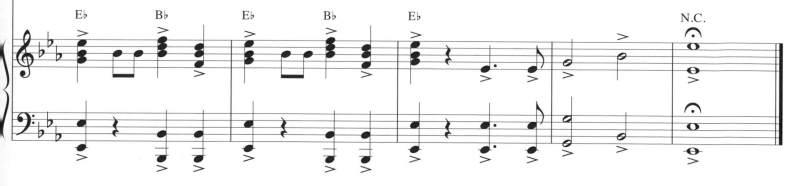

185. EINE KLEINE NACHTMUSIK – Solo *(Concert E♭ version: Flute, Alto Sax.)*

Wolfgang Amadeus Mozart
Arr. by John Higgins

185. EINE KLEINE NACHTMUSIK – Solo *(Concert Bb version: Oboe, Clarinet)*

Wolfgang Amadeus Mozart
Arr. by John Higgins

120

185. THEME FROM SYMPHONY NO. 1 – Solo *(Concert E♭ version: Bsn., Alto Cl., Bar. Sax., Tpt., Tbn., Bar. B.C., Bar. T.C., Tuba)*

Johannes Brahms
Arr. by John Higgins

185. THEME FROM SYMPHONY NO. 1 – Solo *(Concert B♭ version: Bs. Cl., T. Sax., F Horn)*

Johannes Brahms
Arr. by John Higgins

122

186. SWING LOW, SWEET CHARIOT – Duet

African-American Spiritual

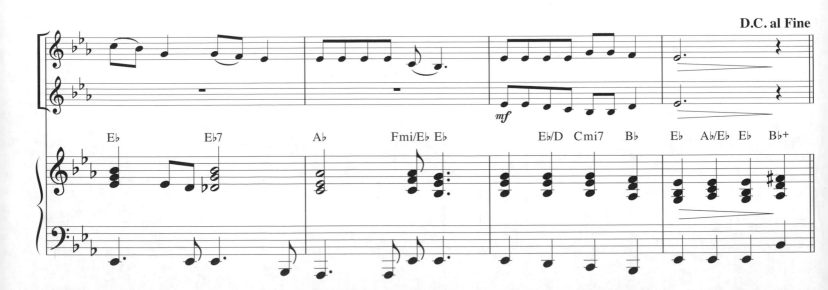

187. LA BAMBA – Duet

Mexican Folk Song

KEY OF CONCERT B♭ MAJOR

1.

2.

3.

4.

KEY OF CONCERT E♭ MAJOR

1.

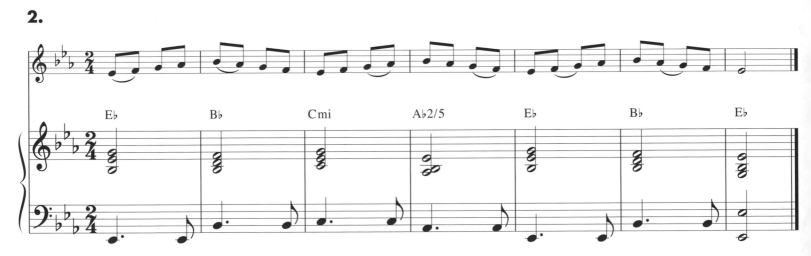

2.

3.

4.

KEY OF CONCERT F MAJOR

1.

KEY OF CONCERT A♭ MAJOR

4.